Stuttering

25 Most Effective Methods and Techniques to Overcome Stuttering

Description

Are you a teen or adult who sometimes stutter or perhaps a professional individual with a stuttering issue? This book **"Stuttering and 25 Most Effective Methods and Techniques to Overcome Stuttering"** describes a list of 25 helpful tips that you can use to avoid stuttering and stammering in your speech. In this book, you will have an overview of the condition and how a person can stop stuttering when speaking. You will learn about some techniques for reducing anxiety which increase the onset of stuttering. You will also learn very useful tips that are helpful for controlling stuttering in children. These methods are helpful for those who have this disorder at birth and also for those who develop it later in life. Finally you will learn about some effective medical treatments for stuttering.

This book will cover the following:

- What is Stuttering
- Techniques to help with stuttering by reducing anxiety
- How to manage Stuttering
- Stuttering in Children
- Medical Solutions

TABLE OF CONTENTS

Introduction 1

Chapter 1 – What is Stuttering 2

Causes Of Stuttering 2

1. Genetic Basis 2

2. A Type Of Tic 3

3. Auditory Processing Deficit 3

Chapter 2 – Techniques to Help With Stuttering By Reducing Anxiety 4

1. Understanding Stuttering 4

2. Try To Overcome It 4

3. Don't Feel Ashamed of Stuttering 5

4. Practice Speech In Front of Friends 5

5. Stop Avoiding Situations Where You Have To Speak 6

6. Address the Behavior Of People Who Make Fun Of You 6

7. Join A Support Group 6

8. Stop Thinking that Stutter Must Go Away Completely 7

Chapter 3 – How To Manage Stuttering and Stammering 8

9. Memorize It 8

10. Speak Comfortably When You Can 8

11. Take As Much Time As You Need 9

12. Make Sure To BREATHE 9

13. Practice Stuttering 10

14. Grasp Difficult Sounds With Easier Ones 10

15. Go To A Therapist 11

16. Electronic Speech Aid 11

Chapter 4 – Tackling Stutter Issues In Children 12

17. Identify Stutter 12

18. Start Speaking Slowly 12

19. Provide A Comfortable Environment For Child 13

20. Let Them Finish What They Say 13

21. Give Parental Feedback 13

Chapter 5 – Medicines For Stuttering 15

22. Placebo Effect 15

23. Alprazolam 15

24.   **Citalopram** 16

25.   **Clomipramine** 16

Conclusion **18**

INTRODUCTION

There are many different disorders that are present in a person naturally at birth. Stuttering is one such disorder. This type of disorder may not have any significant harmful effects on the person nor lead a person to physical disability but this type of disorder present a big obstacle in the personality growth and development of the person and make it very difficult for the person to be successful. It presents difficulties for the person in his career and in his personal life as well. So, it is important that this disorder be addressed at the right time in the most appropriate manner so that it does not affect any aspect of that individual's life.

As far as the stutter is concerned, the medical research that has been carried out up till now does not propose any exact causes for the problem nor does it suggest any exact medicines that guarantee a cure for it. But it does not mean that the problem is not solvable because researchers and experts of the field have suggested various tips and exercises that were found helpful for it.

These tips and exercises address different aspects of the disorder. In the coming chapters, you will learn about these tips. Some of these address the problem directly while others aim to reduce it by targeting its causes. Some of the tips are for reducing the after effects of this problem. It does not matter the way in which these tips and exercises work because the basic purpose is to make sure that they are helpful to those with the disorder. If you are among the many who have this disorder, you should try all the methods that are mentioned in the coming chapters as they will prove highly beneficial for you.

CHAPTER 1 – WHAT IS STUTTERING

Stuttering is a type of disorder in which a person is not able to speak in a fluent manner and his speech involves a lot of disruption. The term is commonly used to refer to constant "disfluencies" when speaking and it can also be used to refer to the difficulty stutterer's face in their communication.

Stuttering not only produce disfluencies but also makes it difficult for the person to use his speech muscles effectively. The affected person may often develop different psychological problems related to embarrassment, fear of speaking, physical tension and anxiety. These symptoms and the already present problem of stuttering make it very difficult for the person to communicate with others in an effective manner. There are many different patterns of stuttering and these may vary from person to person, the severity of stuttering also varies from person to person.

CAUSES OF STUTTERING

The cause of stuttering is still not known however, scientists and researchers have been able to figure out several different causes that can lead to stuttering. A number of theories have been put forward that implies multiple factors that can be the reason for stuttering.

1. GENETIC BASIS

Most of the theories and the results from researches have shown that stuttering in individuals often has its roots in the genetics of a person. Children who have stutter disorder in their family, especially in the first order relatives are observed to have three times more chances of developing a stuttering disorder. From the studies carried out on twins and adopted children, it has been suggested that environmental factors along with genetic factors create a strong reason for stuttering whereas there are a lot of people who stutter without having any family history of this disorder. Some of the genes that are common in people who stutter are GNPTAB, NAGPA, and GNPTG. According to researches, it is observed that about 9% of those people who stutter and have a family history of stuttering have slight modifications in these genes

2. A Type Of Tic

According to some of the researches, it has been reported that stuttering is rather a complex sort of tic. A tic is an involuntary action such as the blinking of eyes etc. A tic is always sudden and it involves some specific muscles of your body for the tic to happen. Most common tics are the clearing of throat and blinking of eyes. There are simple tics and complex tics and stuttering has been classified as one of the complex tics.

A complex tic stays for a longer period of time and is often a meaningless movement. Some of the complex tics are the sudden jerks in your shoulders and similar jerks in your entire body, unknowingly touching objects etc.

3. Auditory Processing Deficit

It has been proposed that auditory processing problems can be one of the reasons behind stuttering. It has been observed that stuttering is not common among deaf people and those for which it is hard to hear. It has also been proposed when the auditory feedback is modified in the people who stutter, they start showing improvements in their speech. The modification can be done by several means such as by delaying the feedback or by masking it in some manner or by changing its frequency. It has also been observed that in some stuttering individuals, the auditory system is a bit different than the people who do not stutter.

CHAPTER 2 – TECHNIQUES TO HELP WITH STUTTERING BY REDUCING ANXIETY

Fear of speaking in public or getting very nervous before going for an interview is something that a lot of people experience. While stuttering is a disorder, one of the major reasons behind it is this sort of fear. The stuttering that comes from the physical disorder can become a lot worse when fear of speech is also there. In the coming sections, you will find out the techniques using which you can avoid stuttering or reduce its severity so that it is easy to listen to and follow your speech. It will help you minimize the impact of stuttering.

1. UNDERSTANDING STUTTERING

It is important that you realize the mechanism of stuttering so that you are able to minimize it. A person keeps getting stuck on one sound when his speech is blocked and this makes him either stuck there or causes him to keep repeating the same sound without being able to complete the word. It happens because the vocal chords of the person apply maximum force and thus they render the person unable to speak. This continues for as long as the tension in the vocal chords is not released. So, the first technique is to understand that as soon as there is first stutter in the speech, you have to stop speaking further and then start again when the tension in your vocal chords is gone. You should not force yourself to complete the word as it will only keep making the situation worse. You need to wait until you are able to speak the word and then complete it. If you are able to do so, you will be able to reduce your anxiety and tackle your stuttering problems.

2. TRY TO OVERCOME IT

If you have a stuttering problem and you really want to minimize its effects then you should know that you are the only one who can do that. You have to be determined and do things that are suggested and you have to understand that although it may be difficult, but if you keep going you will be able to reduce continuous stuttering in your speech. You just have to hang in there and never give up on it and you will start seeing results in a matter of months. But if you give up on it, then it is going to stay there for the rest of your life. You have got to learn how to utter words without stuttering and learning this will take time, patience and determination. So, if you want to overcome it, you have to be strong about it because that is among the most effective methods of reducing the impact of stuttering.

3. DON'T FEEL ASHAMED OF STUTTERING

Stuttering is not something for which you should feel ashamed of. It does not represent anything like your level of intelligence, your personality or the way you were brought up by your guardians. It does not mean that you are an overly anxious or nervous person who has no confidence. Once you realize this, it will help you speak with better fluency and it will also give you the confidence that your positive thinking can help reduce the severity of stuttering. Although feeling bad about it is normal, you have to use this feeling to boost your positive thinking instead of allowing it to make your condition worse. You should not feel ashamed about it, you should not feel ashamed about telling others about it and you should definitely now feel ashamed when people learn that you have it. When you have a weakness, you need to use it as a trait of yourself rather than feeling bad about it.

4. PRACTICE SPEECH IN FRONT OF FRIENDS

A person often feels bad when his shortcomings are noticed by strangers but in case of supportive people, it is not the same. Friends and family members support you and you should make sure that you utilize their support to its maximum extent. Therefore, you should try to practice your speech as much as you can in front of people who are supportive of you. Be open to them about the fact that you are self-conscious about your stuttering and that you want them to help you overcome this problem. You can ask your family members and your friends for their help and support. As for what you need to talk about? well it can be anything, you can just take part in any conversations that they are having or you can read them aloud something from a book or newspaper etc.

5. STOP AVOIDING SITUATIONS WHERE YOU HAVE TO SPEAK

A lot of people who stutter try to conceal the fact and hide it from others for as long as they can, so therefore they speak as little as possible and only where they have no other choice but to speak. This is something that holds you back and has a negative impact on your personality. You have to start facing such situations with confidence. It does not mean that you need to go out of your way and start speaking where it is totally unnecessary. You just have to keep speaking like you would if there was no stutter. Keep having conversations with friends and other supportive people and try not to remove yourself from society, instead go out and face your fears.

6. ADDRESS THE BEHAVIOR OF PEOPLE WHO MAKE FUN OF YOU

If there is a bully putting making fun of you one of the best ways of dealing with them is to simply ignore, but if said bully is a friend making fun of you then let them know that it bothers you. You have to let him know because if you don't, they will continue to offend you thinking that you are okay with you. So, be open about it and tell him that this is something that upset and offend you. Most likely your friend will stop teasing you but if not, it means that you have to start avoiding them. If there are a lot of people in your social circle who make fun of your stuttering, you have to warn them about it and tell them that it upsets you as well as the negative impact it has on you.

7. JOIN A SUPPORT GROUP

If stuttering bothers you a lot and you think that you really need some help, you can join a support group. For this purpose, you can search for one in your area and if there is none, you can always go and join an online forum specifically for people who stutter.

There, you can share your experiences, the problems that you face and the way in which you try to handle them. There will be others who will know exactly the things that you say and knowing that someone truly understands your problem is a very helpful. More than likely you will receive good advice from people in the group. Some of them may even provide techniques to reduce the level of stuttering that you have. There are also National Stuttering Associations in many countries to help people with stuttering disorder. If you find one in your country, if would be especially beneficial to attend the conferences, support groups, or any other gatherings and benefit from the services that are offered for people who stutter.

8. STOP THINKING THAT STUTTER MUST GO AWAY COMPLETELY

You should understand that it is very rare for someone to completely cure his stutter, but that also does not mean that you should give up on minimizing its effects. The more you are able to control your anxiety, the better you are at dealing with your stutter. Sometimes, you may start stammering a lot in your speech even after you have controlled it but that is just temporary and it will go away soon so don't panic, instead keep focusing on minimizing it. If you are good enough in properly convincing people and making your point, you will realize that stutter is completely harmless. Moreover, continuous efforts can make your stutter minimal to almost non-existent.

CHAPTER 3 – HOW TO MANAGE STUTTERING AND STAMMERING

In this chapter, you will learn the techniques of minimizing the stutter by learning how to manage it. Once you learn how to manage it and deal with it in different situations, it will help you to control it in situations where stuttering makes you look unfavorable. Managing the stutter does not mean that you will be able to get rid of it for good. It means that you will be able to keep it under control when you are in a meeting or interview etc.

9. MEMORIZE IT

It has been observed that people who stutter in their everyday speech do not face this problem when they are reading some passage or when they are singing a tune from a song that they have memorized. So, one of the techniques of managing the stutter is to speak some of the sentences from your memory. These could be the sentences that you verbalize frequently in your speech. It will soon become a part of your involuntary speaking actions. It may not be helpful to all but for some individuals this practice will prove to be very effective.

10. SPEAK COMFORTABLY WHEN YOU CAN

Without any stutter, you need to continue going on like that without trying to make any effort. You should not try to make any changes in the way you are speaking for as long as you can go without encountering stutter. This way, you will be able to go on without stammering for longer and longer periods of time. While you are speaking, instead of thinking about stuttering, just think about what it is that you have to say and say it in the most comfortable manner. You should not get worried about whether you will be able to say it all without having to stop in the middle of the sentence. Try it and you will realize that it is one of the very effective ways of dealing with a stuttering disorder in your speech. Your period of continuous sentences will keep improving this way and the stutter in your speech will be greatly decreased.

11. TAKE AS MUCH TIME AS YOU NEED

A great practice is to stop and not try to force a word out if you are getting stuck at saying it. Instead of trying to blurt the word out, you need to slow down, take your time and then say it when you feel like you are ready to say it. It's the same as when you try to speak when having food in your mouth but you wait until you swallow before you are able to say the word. You should wait until you feel that your vocal chords are ready to say what you are trying to say and so that your words come out smooth and easily. This will help with anxiety that causes you to stutter and that you feel after stuttering. When you take a pause, be aware that most sensible people listening to you will not take it as a bad thing, so you shouldn't worry about what they might think.

12. MAKE SURE TO BREATHE

Whenever a person who stutters gets stuck on a word, he tries to hold his breath and say the word out loud i.e. force it out of his mouth as if there is no other choice. If you also have the stuttering disorder, you will notice this the next time you stutter but your response should be different. What you don't realize is that such problems only make it more difficult to speak. What needs to be done in these situations is to make sure that pause, take a deep breath and try to say the word while exhaling. It will help with your speech and it will also allow you to minimize stuttering. You might face difficulty trying to do this in your first attempts but as you keep practicing, you will keep getting better at it. All you have to do is make sure that trying to speak does not hinder your breathing and if it does, just pause and try again when you are exhaling.

...e of the ways in which you can try to manage your
... Try to practice stuttering when you are alone and
...d sounds that you think are difficult for you to say.
...l of your speech. For example, if you are not able to
...rt practicing it by saying "G-g-g-great". When you do
... getting better at it. When you do this, you won't be
...use you will be practicing. You will try to say it without
...nd you will do it in a calm and continuous manner with
...tter kicks in, you can just repeat the process until you
...d easily. Practice it with a bunch of words that are
...you will keep getting better. It is just like when you do a
... to figure out your weaknesses and overcome them when
you still have the time.

14.   GRASP DIFFICULT SOUNDS WITH EASIER ONES

Most of the times a person knows that there are certain sounds at which he stutters and some people start to feel the pressure when they know that sound is coming next in their speech. It feels like an obstacle or a wall that hinders their flow of speech, but the good thing is that you can get over this obstacle by using a simple technique. You have to try and skip the difficult sounds and replace them with ones that you can easily produce. For example, if you are not able to say "dog" due to a stutter in producing sound of a D, you can try using "The" sound instead of it. Same way, you can keep figuring out the sounds that are easier for you to produce in place of ones that initiate stutter in your speech. For example, you can use "aaa" in place of "mm" sound and it will just deliver almost same sound. This trick will prove helpful in many situations and you should practice it often. This practice is similar to changing your accent a bit.

15.   GO TO A THERAPIST

You can greatly minimize the effects of stuttering i.e. the anxiety and stress it causes and stuttering itself if you get help from a speech therapist. The thing is that most people have different stuttering patterns and if you go to the therapist, he will be able to analyze your pattern in detail and then he will be able to guide you based on the results. Your speech therapist will tell you special exercises that can minimize stuttering in your speech. You should realize that it will not entirely go away, but that it will be greatly reduced. You may find some of the practices and therapies devised by the therapist a bit difficult but you need to hang in there with patience and you will soon start seeing positive results.

If you don't see any visible results even after practicing with a certain therapist for quite some time, you should try a different therapist. Sometimes there maybe therapists who might suggest exercises and techniques that can actually make the problem worse.

16.   ELECTRONIC SPEECH AID

If stutter continues to persist and make you anxious and nervous, you can always try some electronic speech aid. For this purpose, you can either buy a special-purpose device or you can use some other general purpose device like a recording tool that is designed to allow you to hear the way you speak. The few drawbacks of this particular technique are that some of these devices are rather expensive and you won't be able to use them effectively in public places where there is noise and other distractions. Despite the few drawbacks of electronics speech aids, it is still a good technique that may be useful for coping with stutter problems.

CHAPTER 4 – TACKLING STUTTER ISSUES IN CHILDREN

Stutter problems in children should be identified and tackled as early as possible because it can help in controlling the level of stutter and reducing its severity. For this reason, some basic techniques and tips provided should not be avoided. If done properly, the child will be able to not only control his stutter but he will also be able to deal with problems that are caused as a result of it.

17.   IDENTIFY STUTTER

In children, it is sometimes difficult to identify problems, especially speech problems because they are still learning to speak properly. But if you try to identify, you will be easily able to distinguish between the problems that are due to learning process and stutter problems. So, if you think there is any sort of stuttering in your child's speech never ignore it. Sometimes, the stutter goes away with time but it does not mean that you should not take appropriate steps for the betterment of your child. If you don't take action then chances are the stuttering may get worse and may become permanent. So try to tackle it in the early and take all the steps that you can to prevent it from getting worse.

18.   START SPEAKING SLOWLY

If you identify a stammering problem in your child, try to slow down your speech. The reason is that children learn by copying the adults and when you are speaking too fast, it can be difficult for them to say the words at the same rate as you. This may lead them to stutter as they try to utter words with maximum speed. So, make sure to use easy words with them that are easy on the tongue and vocal chords, also avoid speaking too fast. Maintain a rhythm in your speech, especially when you are talking to children and also when you are talking to someone in front of them. This can be a bit difficult for you, but it will mean a lot for them.

19. PROVIDE A COMFORTABLE ENVIRONMENT FOR CHILD

Your child should have a comfortable and relaxed environment where he can speak easily without having to face any sort of pressure. You should make sure that he gets all the time that he needs to say whatever it is that he needs to say. Listen to him when he is speaking and do not interrupt him as that can lower his confidence and self-esteem. Try to take time out of your activities when your child wants to speak and give him your full attention so that he knows that when he is speaking, somebody listens to him. It will give him the feeling that his stuttered speech is not annoying for others. On the other hand, if you do not properly listen to him, he will just try to avoid any situations where there is a need to speak. This will not only make them less willing to speak but also increase his levels of anxiety.

20. LET THEM FINISH WHAT THEY SAY

As mentioned above, to boost the confidence of children and reduce the feeling of anxiety and stress, you should allow them to complete their sentences. Be supportive to them when they are speaking but be sure to not finish their sentences for them as it can give them a feeling of needing support every time they talk. It is more of a psychological problem and you should understand that if you are ready to treat it in its early stage, it can save the child a lot of embarrassment in his own mind. So, do not walk away when they are talking and try not to interrupt or make them feel that you are in haste when they get stuck at a word.

21. GIVE PARENTAL FEEDBACK

The technique of parental feedback to help control developmental stuttering in children was developed a few decades ago. In this technique, a therapist teaches the parents or guardians of the children the different ways that can help the child with his problem. In this method, they do not get the child to enroll in the program because that can make him feel that he has a disorder. So, they tell parents about it and parents take the necessary steps to control stuttering problem of their child. Some of the ways in which you can help your child are as follows.

- Do not talk to the child about stammering if he does not want you to.
- When the child is able to speak long sentences without stuttering, appreciate him in a way that does not draw too much attention but makes him feel like he has achieved something. For example, you can just pat him and say "Great!" etc.
- Try to make sure that you never point out the stutter as something that is annoying and especially avoid mentioning it when a child is feeling down and depressed.

CHAPTER 5 – MEDICINES FOR STUTTERING

Most of the research that has been done until now suggests that stuttering is a disorder related to the development of the person and there is no medication that can be used to totally cure it. Rather than using medication, they try to handle this problem as a psychological issue that should be treated with therapy.

22.   PLACEBO EFFECT

In one of the researches that were conducted, a group of people with stuttering issues were asked to undergo some drugs that were supposed to help with their stutter. Half of these people were given actual medicine while the other halves were placed under the placebo effect. At the end of the studies, it was shown that both groups showed same levels of improvement which further proved the point that the issue has its roots in psychology.

However, it does not mean that there are not any medicines that can effectively work against this problem. In recent years, some published reports claimed that three drugs, i.e. Alprazolam, Citalopram, and Clomipramine can help in reducing stuttering.

None of these drugs however can be taken without a prescription from a registered health care professional.

23.   ALPRAZOLAM

Alprazolam is a famous drug that goes by the name Xanax. It has some other generic uses as well. It has properties of a sedative, muscle relaxant and an anxiolytic. It is a medically approved drug used for anxiety, panic disorders and social anxiety disorder. It also has the properties of an amnestic.

Alprazolam acts fast and mostly its effects can be observed one hour after taking the dose.

Research showed that Alprazolam has been beneficial for stuttering patient and made them lose most of the stutter in their speech. This action of Alprazolam can be directly linked to its anxiolytic properties because when it reduces anxiety in the person, he is able to speak in a more clear tone as it gives them more confidence to speak.

24. CITALOPRAM

Citalopram is a registered drug to be taken in case of depression and for some other conditions as well. It is also used for panic disorders. There are a lot of side-effects associated with this drug such as palpitating heartbeat, endocrine effects and adverse effects in case of pregnancy. Increased use of Citalopram can lead a person to suicidal behavior and thinking. So it is very important to use it only if prescribed by a registered health care professional. It has many different brand names in different countries throughout the world

As for the applications of Citalopram in case of stuttering, it is shown that it can help in selective patients. Some of them are reported to show very good results while others may show only a slight betterment.

Some patients suggested mild improvements while others complained of the side effects while using Citalopram for the treatment of stuttering.

25. CLOMIPRAMINE

Clomipramine is the third drug that has been reported to help in case of stutter disorder. It is an antidepressant. Its worldwide use began in the 60s when it was first discovered. There are a number of uses of this drug which includes Obsessive Compulsive Disorder, Panic Disorder, Major Depressive Disorder, Chronic Pain and various other disorders. There are quite a number of adverse effects associated with the usage of Clomipramine. These include dizziness, weight loss or weight gain, restlessness, palpitations, hallucinations, abdominal problems and many other health issues. An overdose can lead to some severe symptoms and possible even a coma so it is highly recommended that

Clomipramine be used only when prescribed. Two out of Three people however, reported that Clomipramine stood out as the drug with the least side effects.

These tests were carried out under the supervision of John Paul Brady and Zahir Ali at Merion, Pennsylvania Elmhurst, New York.

CONCLUSION

From all the studies that have been carried out so far, it has been observed that although there is no medicine available as of now for the disorder, there are still some therapies that are highly beneficial. Stuttering in itself is not something that can inflict pain on the person who suffers from it. Rather, it affects the personality of the person and has more psychological effects than physical ones.

If stuttering is something that bothers you, there are a lot of exercises and therapies that can help you with this problem. You can keep working on these different exercises and there are some drugs as well that are reported to reduce it, but they are not yet approved by the FDA. It is best to only use medications that have been approved. As for reducing the intensity and severity of the issue, the tips mentioned in the previous chapters have been proven to be extremely helpful for most sufferers. Most of these tips require the person to actively work on them with full devotion, determination, and focus. If you keep working at it, you will see a lot of improvements in your speech and you will also feel that you are able to communicate your thoughts to others in a more confident tone.

Made in the USA
Columbia, SC
30 August 2020